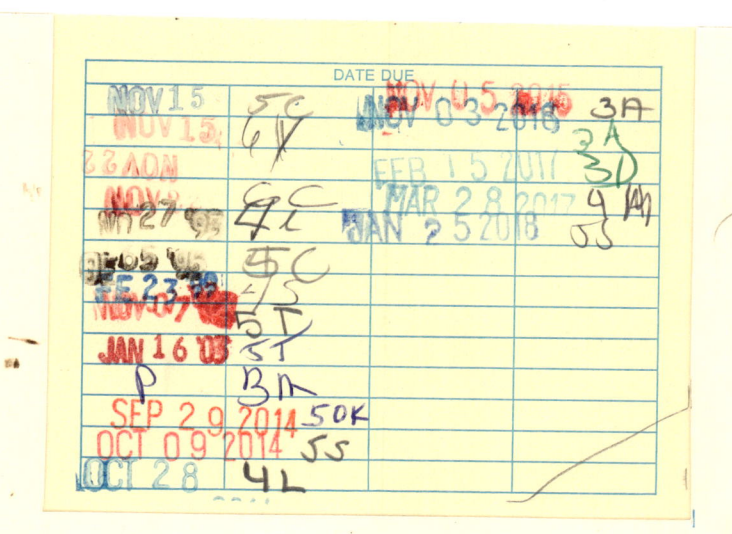

796.332 Allen, James.
ALL
       Football, play like
       a pro.

7592

**SEYMOUR SCHOOL MEDIA CENTER
EAST GRANBY, CT 06026**

870786 01028 50540D 02180F

Be the Best
FOOTBALL

Play Like a Pro
By James Allen

Troll Associates

Library of Congress Cataloging-in-Publication Data
Allen, James, (date)
    Football, play like a pro / by James Allen.
       p.   cm.—(Be the best!)
    Summary: Explains football basics and suggests a few drills.
    ISBN 0-8167-1929-2 (lib. bdg.)   ISBN 0-8167-1930-6 (pbk.)
    1. Football—Juvenile literature. [1. Football.]   I. Title.
    II. Series.
    GV950.7.A45   1990
    796.332'2—dc20   89-38633

Copyright © 1990 by Troll Associates, Mahwah, New Jersey
All rights reserved. No part of this book may be used or reproduced in any manner whatsoever without written permission from the publisher.
Printed in the United States of America.
10 9 8 7 6 5 4 3 2 1

Be the Best
FOOTBALL

Play Like a Pro

FOREWORD
by Jack Bicknell

I've played and coached football for many years. I know what it's like to win, and I know what it's like to lose. Win or lose, though, I've always loved the game itself. I think football provides a thrill no other sport can match.

This book on football does an excellent job of presenting the basics. It gives a short history of the game, explains its rules, and offers sound tips on actual play. The book also describes drills you can do to improve the football skills you'll learn. I recommend it without reservation.

Jack Bicknell

Jack Bicknell has been head football coach for the Boston College Eagles since 1981. In that time, he has coached the Eagles to four post-season bowl games. In 1984, Boston College quarterback Doug Flutie won the Heisman Trophy, and the Eagles finished fourth in a national football poll. That ranking was the highest in history for Boston College. In 1985, Jack Bicknell was selected as head coach of the East squad in Hawaii's Hula Bowl. Aside from Boston College, Jack was head football coach at the University of Maine for five years.

Contents

Chapter	Title	Page
1	Football's Family Tree	7
2	What You Need to Play Football	11
3	The Game in General	15
4	Developing Football Skills	23
5	Football Positions	29
6	Offensive Play	33
7	Defensive Play	45
8	Football Drills	53
9	Touch Football	61
10	Sportsmanship	63

Football's Family Tree

What is the world's most rugged sport? Many people would say football. Football is a rough-and-tumble game of strength, skill, and speed. It is exciting to watch and play.

Football is America's favorite fall sport, and it is certainly among the most popular sports in the country. The game is played mostly in the United States and Canada. But its popularity is beginning to stretch across the ocean. Football teams can now be found in such countries as England and Italy.

The roots of American football also stretch across the ocean. It is descended from the game of soccer. In fact, the game of soccer is known as football in most countries around the world.

How football evolved from soccer is an interesting story. It happened in England in the year 1823. Boys at Rugby School in central England were playing a game of soccer.

EARLY RUGBY STYLE FOOTBALL

A player named William Webb Ellis did something no one expected. When the ball came to him, Ellis scooped it up in his hands and ran down the field. The other players were shocked and surprised. Picking up a soccer ball and running with it is strictly against the rules.

The other players tried to get the ball back by tackling

Ellis. They had so much fun trying to stop the ball carrier that they decided to change the rules of their game. That is how traditional soccer accidentally gave birth to a brand-new sport. The sport was named Rugby after the school where the game was invented. In Rugby, players are allowed to kick or run with the ball.

In 1871, a football game that combined kicking and carrying the ball began in the United States. A group of Harvard athletes was the first American team to experiment with the new Rugby-style football game.

A short time later, several colleges formed an Intercollegiate Football Association to play Rugby football. Members of this association included Columbia, Princeton, and Yale. The association established football's first official rules.

The person who did the most to change English Rugby into American football was Walter Camp. Camp was a player and coach for the Yale team. He helped establish key rules, such as a starting line of scrimmage, a series of downs, and a limit of eleven players per team on the field.

From 1880 to 1890, American football continued to change and improve. But the one part of the game that hasn't changed much is the rough nature of play. There was very little protective equipment in the early days. Most players played without helmets or pads. So many serious injuries followed that President Theodore Roosevelt almost banned the sport of football. But football experts saved the game by outlawing dangerous plays and tactics.

In the 1900s, football became more like the modern game. A touchdown was increased from four points to six points and a field goal was reduced from five points to three points. That shifted the game's emphasis from kicking the ball to running it. In 1906, the forward pass was introduced to the game. It made football even more exciting.

PASSING THE FOOTBALL

Over the years, the game of football has continued to change for the better. Most important, the equipment that protects football players has been vastly improved. Even though there is still the risk of injury, the game is now safer than ever.

Organized football is one sport that requires the help of a qualified coach to learn correctly. However, this book will introduce you to the basics of football. It will show you drills and methods to develop your football skills. So have fun learning about one of America's favorite sports.

What You Need To Play Football

FOOTBALL PHYSICAL

Football is a physically demanding sport. No one should think about playing organized football without first having a thorough physical examination by a medical doctor. *This is a must!*

The doctor should be advised about the purpose of the examination. After you have been given a clean bill of health, you can begin getting the equipment and developing the skills you'll need to play the game.

FOOTBALL PHYSICAL—A MUST!

PROTECTIVE EQUIPMENT

Football is a contact sport. Because of its rugged nature, players wear special protective equipment. Outfitting a football player can be expensive. The total cost of equipment for each player may reach several hundred dollars.

Football games that involve tackling and blocking should *never* be played without proper protective equipment.

Jersey Football players wear jerseys. These are loose-fitting pullover shirts. Most jerseys are numbered according to the players' positions. See pages 29-32 for the different positions in football.

FOOTBALL HELMET

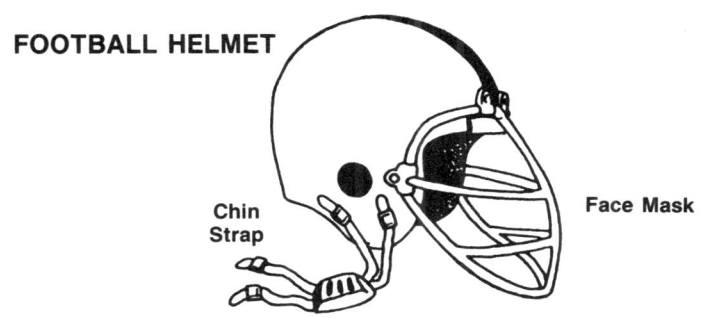

Helmet Football helmets are made of hard plastic. Special foam-, water-, and air-filled chambers inside the helmet help absorb the shock of impact. Bars called a *face mask* protrude from the front and protect a player's face and nose. A cushioned *chin strap* helps secure the helmet. A coach or trainer should initially fit you with a helmet to make sure it is snug and doesn't slip or slide.

Mouthpiece High-school players are required to wear rubber or plastic mouth guards to protect their teeth.

SHOULDER PADS

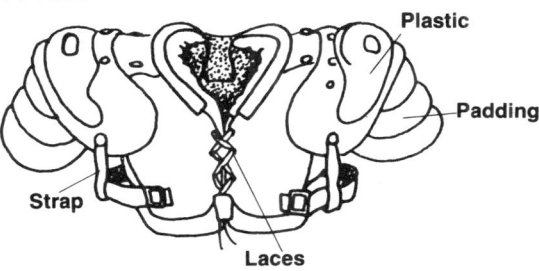

Shoulder pads Shoulder pads are worn over the shoulders and parts of the upper torso. They are made of pads and pieces of stiff, lightweight plastic. They are held by straps that fasten under the player's arms. Shoulder pads, like helmets, should be initially fitted by a coach or trainer.

Hip pads Hip pads or girdle pads protect the hip bones and the lower part of the spine.

FOOTBALL PANTS AND PADS

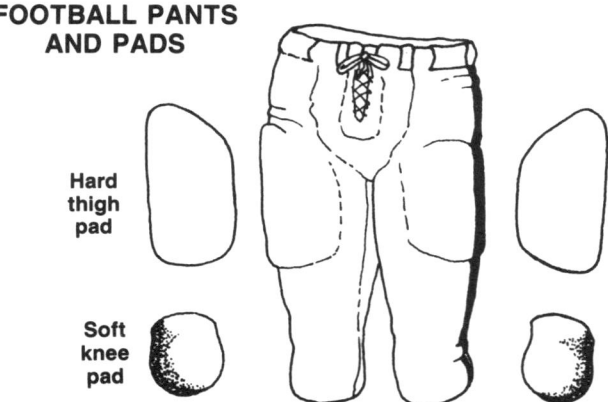

Hard thigh pad

Soft knee pad

Pants Football pants are special, tight-fitting stretch pants with inside compartments for pads. Stiff hard pads are worn over the thigh areas of the legs. Thin, flexible rubber pads are worn over the knees.

Shoes The shoes worn by football players have special spikes. These are plastic or hard rubber with metal tips. Spiked shoes will help you grip the playing surface and improve your footing.

FOOTBALL SHOES

Ball A football is oval shaped and weighs between fourteen and fifteen ounces. It is inflated to a pressure of twelve and a half to thirteen and a half pounds. It is usually a leather-covered, tan or brown ball with white stripes.

The Game in General

The object of a football game is simple. One team of eleven players tries to score more points than the opposing team of eleven players. To score, a team advances the ball down a rectangular field with end and side boundaries. One team advances the ball in one direction. The other team goes in the opposite direction. Teams go up and down the field during play.

Several yards before both end boundaries are goal lines. The area between the goal line and the end boundary is called the end zone. Above the end lines and supported by poles are horseshoe-shaped posts called goal posts.

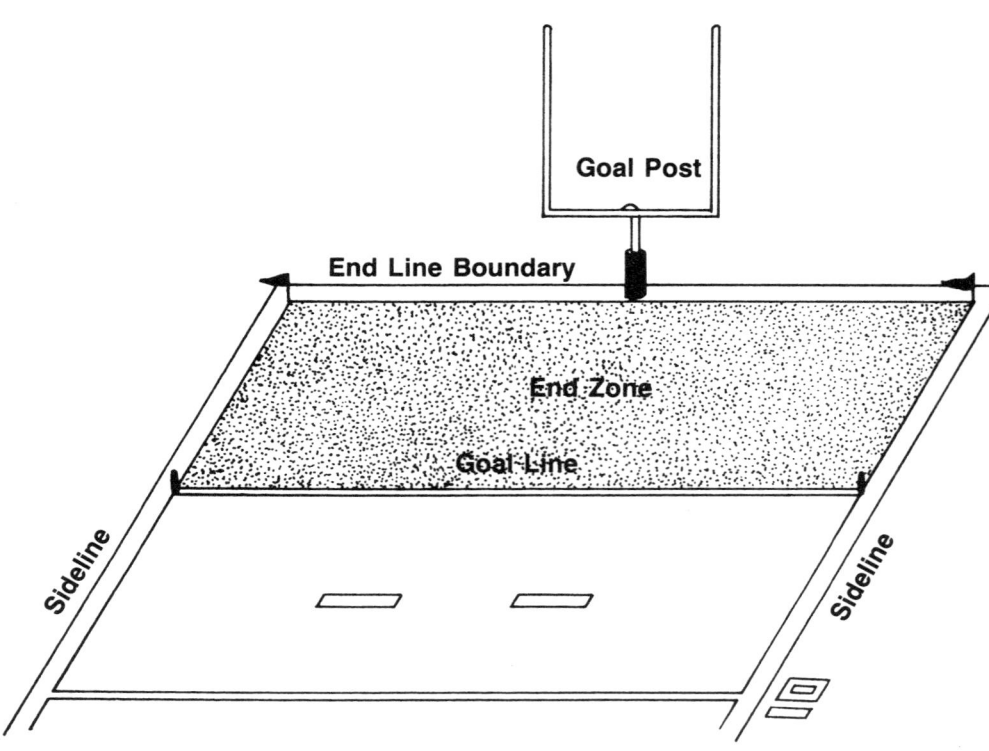

The team with the ball tries to run or pass the ball over the goal line into their opponent's end zone. That team is on offense.

The team without the ball attempts to prevent the advance of the ball. That team is called the defense.

The offense gets four tries, or downs, to advance the ball ten yards from a starting point. If they do so, the offense gets a first down, or four new tries to go an additional ten yards. That sequence continues down the field all the way to the goal line. The offense can run or throw and catch the ball to move it forward. Some players on offense catch the ball or run with it. Others block, or use their bodies to shield the ball carrier from the defensive players. Offensive plays are usually complex.

Each offensive player has a special job on each play.

If the offense does not move the ball ten yards in four downs, the opposing team takes possession of the ball. The teams then switch roles of offense and defense. And the ball moves in the opposite direction.

The defense can also get hold of the ball by intercepting a pass or by recovering a fumble, which is a dropped ball.

Actual scoring is done several ways. A ball run over the goal line or a pass completed in the end zone is called a touchdown. A touchdown is worth six points. After a touchdown, a team is entitled to try for one extra point, or a point after touchdown.

A TOUCHDOWN BEING SCORED

To score the extra point, a team must kick a ball placed on the ground over the bottom bar of the goal posts (see illustration, page 22) and through the two upright posts. The kick is tried from a position near their goal line.

During play, an offensive team may elect to kick the ball through the goal post from a position far from the goal line. That is called a field goal. A field goal is worth three points. A field goal is tried when a team cannot get a touchdown or a first down.

If an offensive team cannot get a first down and is too far away to try a field goal, they must punt on fourth down. A punt is a special kick. A player drops the ball from his hands and boots it downfield. The object of a punt is to give the opposing team the ball far away from their goal line.

The defensive team can prevent the advance of the ball in several ways. A passed ball can be batted away or intercepted before an offensive player catches it. If the pass is caught or a player runs with the ball, the ball carrier must be tackled, or downed. Ball carriers are tackled when they are physically pulled down or knocked off their feet and onto the ground.

**BALL CARRIER
BEING TACKLED**

Where a ball carrier's knee touches the ground is the spot where the next play begins. The ball is placed there. That is the line of scrimmage. It is an imaginary line across the field. The offense must stay on their side of the line of scrimmage and the defense must stay on the other side until play begins.

Play in football is not continuous. It begins with the snap of the ball on offense and ends with an incompleted pass, a tackle, a ball carrier going out of bounds, or a score. There's a brief pause in the action until the next play. Each play is a down unless a rule has been broken.

TIME

Football games are divided into two halves of thirty minutes apiece. Each half is made up of two fifteen-minute quarters. After two quarters of play, there is a fifteen-minute break called halftime. After halftime, the teams switch direction on the field.

KICKOFFS

Each half of a football game starts with a kickoff. The team that will go on defense kicks the ball to the receiving team. The receiving team becomes the offense after returning the kickoff.

The ball is kicked off from the thirty-five-yard line. The receiving team catches it and advances it as far as it can up the field. Play is stopped when the ball carrier is tackled. The spot where the player is tackled becomes the starting line of scrimmage.

Kickoffs also occur after each score. The scoring team kicks off.

FOOTBALL FIELD

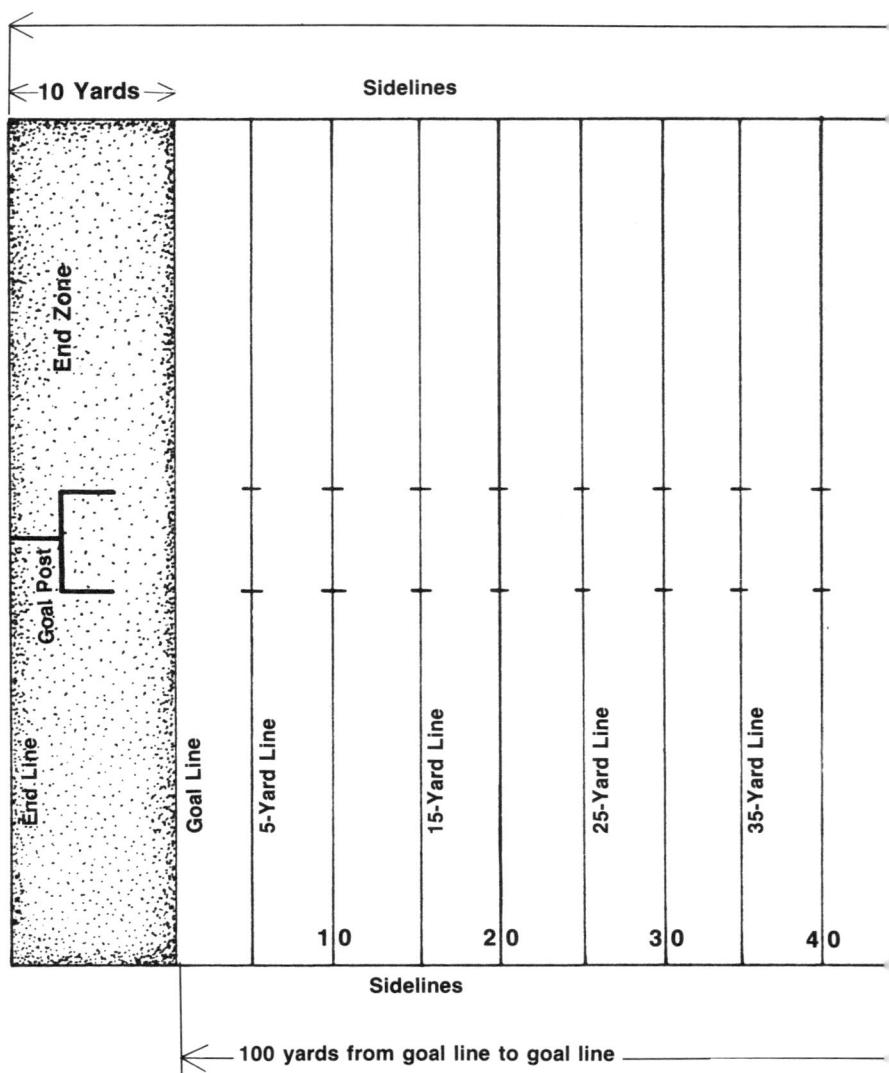

FIELD

A football field is 120 yards long and 53⅓ yards wide. The field from goal line to goal line measures one hundred yards. Each end zone area is ten yards deep.

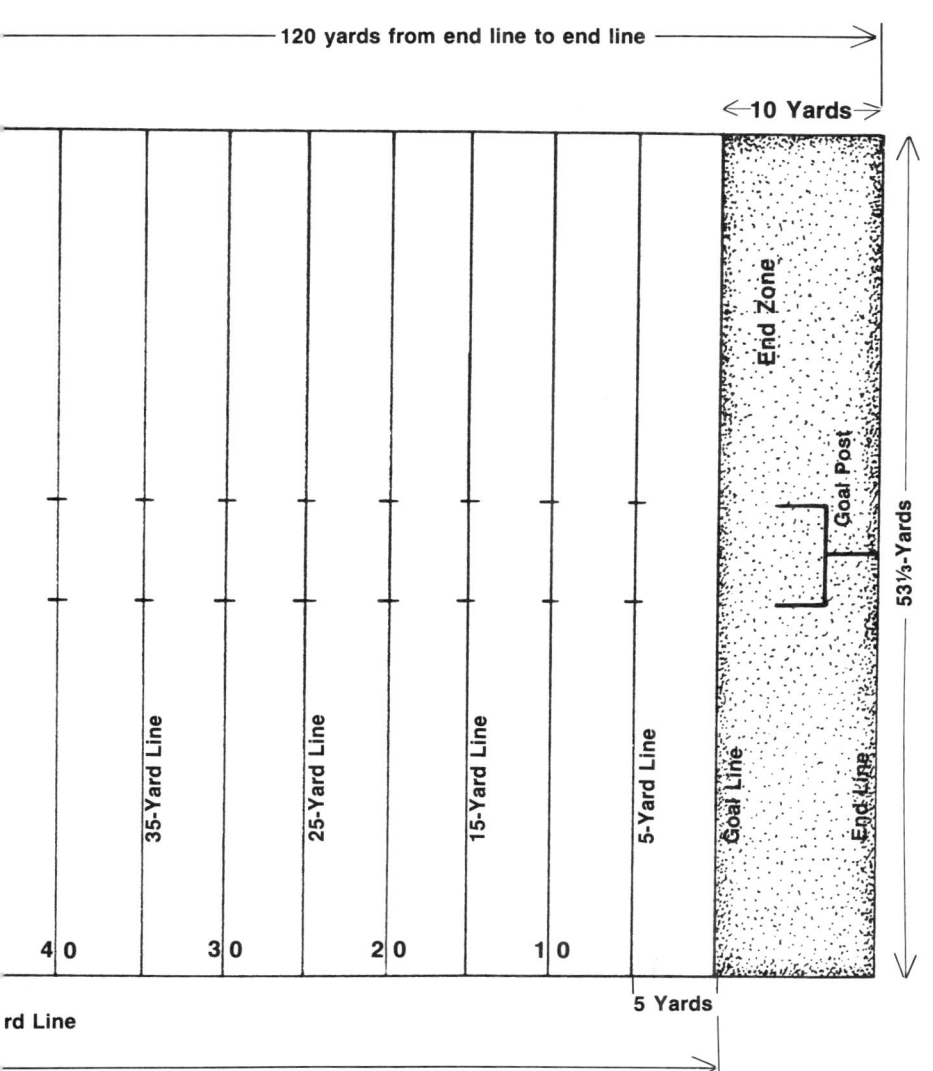

White stripes are painted across the field every five yards. The middle stripe is the fifty-yard line. From the goal line, the stripes are numbered from five to fifty.

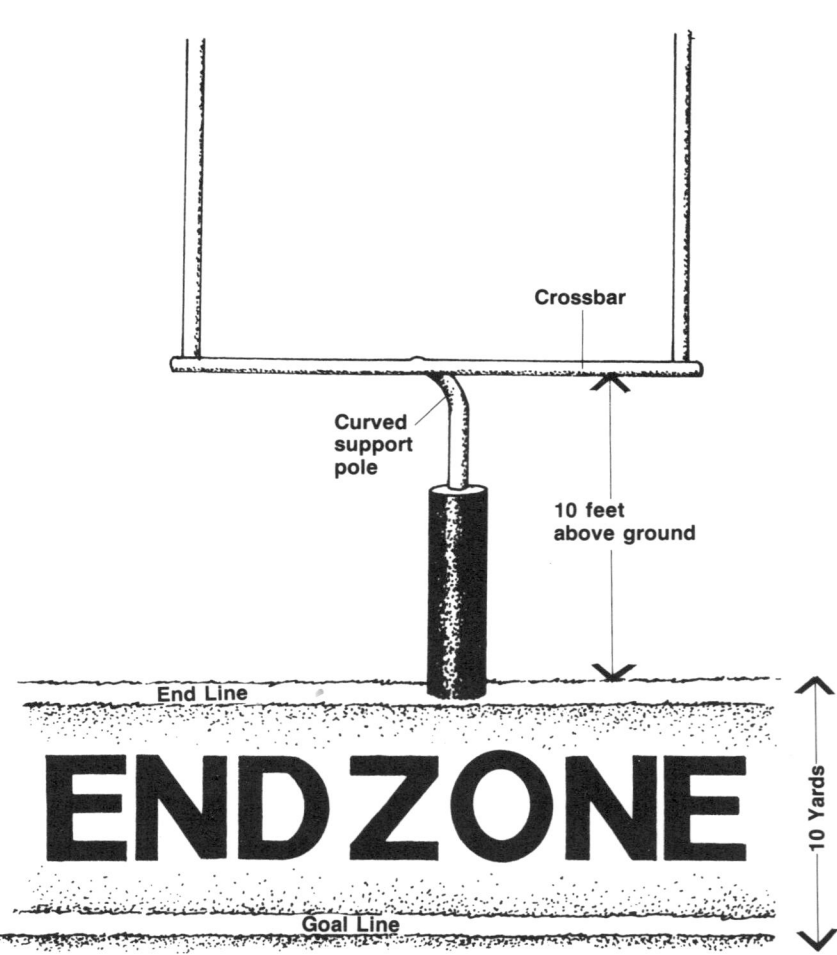

GOAL POSTS

Goal posts are located at opposite ends of the field. They are centered in the middle of the field. A curved support pole on the end line places the goal post above the end zone. The crossbar part of the goal post is ten feet above the ground.

Developing Football Skills

MENTAL TOUGHNESS

Sometimes called a winning attitude, this is a special frame of mind all football players should develop. It combines motivation and determination. With this attitude, football players are mentally tough. They are ready to handle almost any situation on the field. And those sitting on the bench must also be mentally tough so they can enter a game in progress and perform well right away. Mental toughness is often the difference between victory and defeat.

STANCE

Different positions in football use various football stances, or starting positions. However, the stance most players use at one time or another is the three-point stance.

FOOTBALL STANCE—TO GET INTO 3-POINT STANCE

To get into a three-point stance, stand with your feet spread about shoulder width. If you are right-handed, slide your right foot back (reverse if left-handed). The toe of your right foot should be even with your left heel or instep. (Some advanced players move their right foot farther back as a matter of comfort.)

As your foot goes back, bend at the waist while lowering your right hand to the ground. Keep your right elbow locked, and do not lean too far forward on your hand. Stay in a balanced position. The fingers of your support hand should form a tiny tripod with the thumb and first two fingers.

3-POINT STANCE

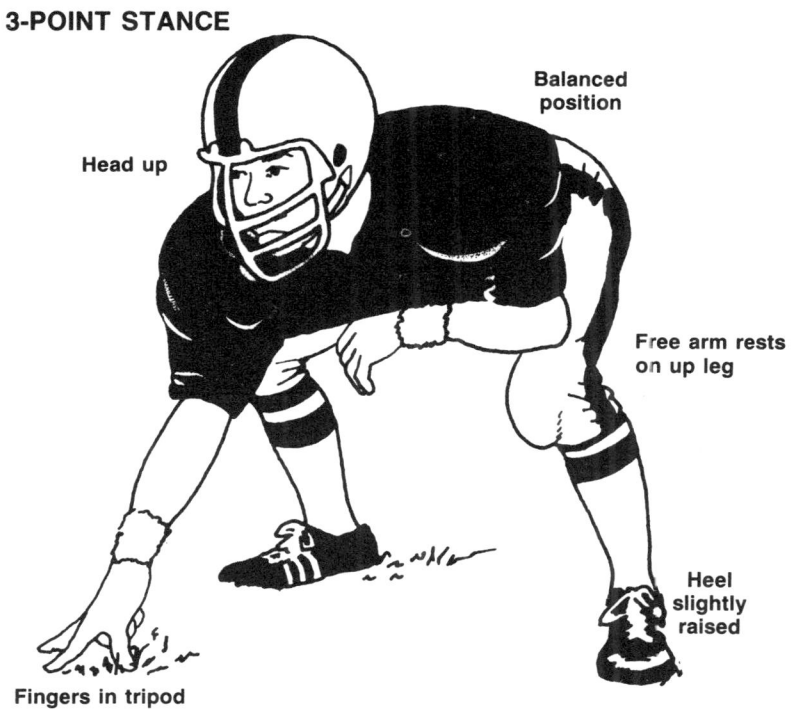

When you're in a three-point stance, keep your chin up. Rest your free arm on the knee of your left leg, or keep the free arm bent and cocked. Do not get your backside too high or too low. It should be almost the same height as your shoulders. Remember to stay balanced. The heel of your right foot will be slightly off the ground. Your left foot should be firmly planted.

CONDITIONING

CONDITIONING

Preseason football work should include calisthenics, distance running, and sprints. Weightlifting and other forms of weight training are *not* recommended for young players.

Calisthenics Football players should do exercises that strengthen the upper body, the legs, and the abdomen. Exercises like pushups, sit-ups, leg lifts, and knee bends are good. Chin-ups or pull-ups are also good builders of upper body strength.

Together, these exercises are called calisthenics. When you do an exercise once, it is called a repetition. A number of repetitions (10-20) make up a set. Calisthenics should be done in sets. You should try to do these exercises in three sets, resting between each one.

Distance Running Distance running builds endurance and stamina. A workout should include distance running and sprints (see next section). Run a few (2-3) distance laps to start your workout. That will loosen up your muscles. Then do sprint work. Finish with more distance laps (4-6). A distance lap should be at least one time around both goal posts if you're on a football field (about a quarter of a mile).

When distance running, pump your arms comfortably. Do not clench your hands into fists, which will slow you down and tire you faster. Relax and breathe through your mouth and nose. Try to make smooth strides and run on the balls, or fronts, of your feet.

Sprints Quick starts and short bursts of speed are crucial in football. And sprints will help you develop both. When you run a sprint, you're usually running at top speed over a given distance. It can be short (10-20 yards), medium (40-50 yards), or long (80-100 yards).

Begin in a three-point stance (see page 24). Take your first step with your back foot. Push off with your front foot, and stay low.

SPRINTS

To loosen up your leg muscles, run your first sprint or two at half speed. Once you feel loose, run the remainder at full speed. When you pass the finish line, gradually slow down to a jog. Then turn and jog back to the starting line. Rest there for a few seconds to catch your breath. Then get down into your three-point stance and sprint again.

A typical workout of sprints might include eight short and eight medium ones, or eight medium and four to six long ones. But *never* run more than you can, and *never* run if you feel ill or woozy.

Football Positions

Which position should you play? To pick your position, be honest with yourself. Examine the qualities you have as an athlete. Then examine the physical demands of various football positions. The closer your athletic qualities are to the physical demands of the position, the better chance you have of playing it.

Your coach will also help you select the best position for you. It may or may not be the position you want to play. But a coach knows how best to use your skills as a football player. Remember, in football your size and weight are important factors at certain positions.

OFFENSIVE TEAM

Center The center is very important—in fact, the key person on the offensive line. The line is built around the center, who has a twofold job. First, the center must snap, or hike, the ball to the quarterback to start play. (How to snap the ball is discussed under "Center Snap" on pages 37-38.) Second, the center must also block.

Centers are usually strong and agile. They are also team leaders.

Offensive Guards and Tackles The unsung heroes of football, offensive guards and tackles are big, strong, and can control their emotions. They must also have the ability to memorize plays and work well as part of a unit. Guards are usually stocky, quick, and mobile. Tackles are very big and strong. They must be able to fire out, that is, move forward quickly while keeping low.

Quarterback The quarterback is the team leader, the player who is in charge and calls the offensive plays. Quarterbacks must be good all-around athletes. They must be able to handle the ball well and to pass both short and long passes. A quarterback knows where all backs and receivers go on each play. That's why a quarterback must be intelligent and cool under pressure. Quick feet, good reactions, and the ability to make split-second decisions are necessary.

Running Backs Running backs need good speed. They must be agile, have good balance, and be able to shift directions swiftly. Stamina and determination are also important. Time and time again, a running back must strive for extra yardage without tiring.

Receivers Ends and flankers are receivers. To be a receiver, you must have good hands. If you cannot catch the ball consistently, you cannot be a receiver. Speed is also a factor. Receivers must be fearless. They must catch the ball without worrying about getting hit. Running good pass patterns and having good concentration are also pluses.

OFFENSIVE FORMATION

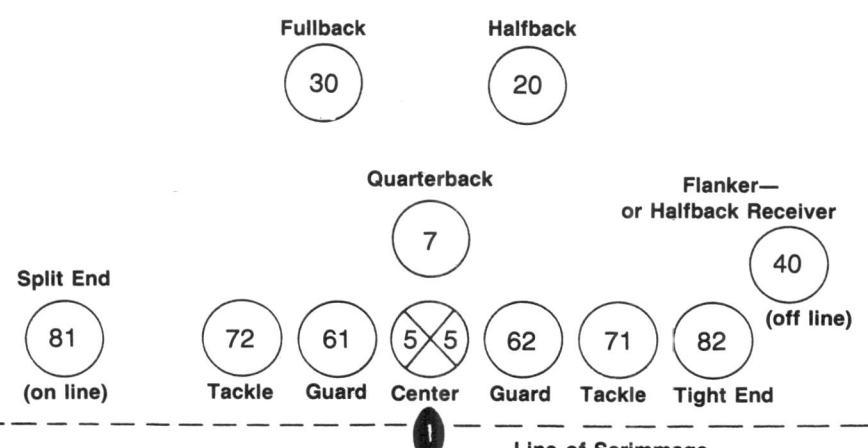

DEFENSIVE TEAM

Linebackers Linebackers are usually the team's toughest players. They are strong and quick. They play against the pass and the run. Linebackers are hard hitters and enjoy contact. They must also have good side-to-side movement.

DEFENSIVE FORMATION

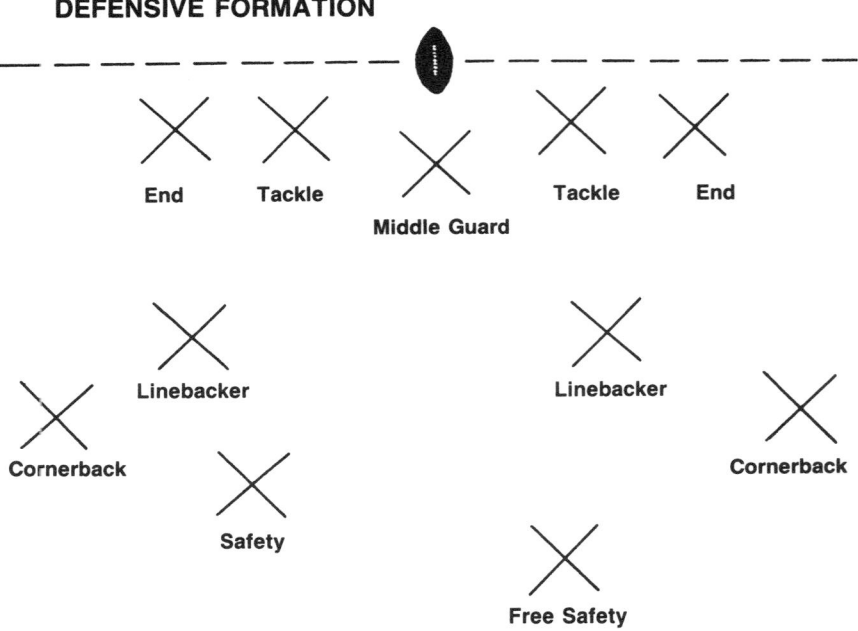

Defensive Guards and Tackles Big and quick, defensive guards and tackles are also agile. They play against the run and rush in on the passer.

Defensive Backs Often the best athletes on the team, defensive backs play mostly against the pass. They are usually small, swift, and independent. Defensive backs tackle well and have good hands.

Offensive Play

The goal of a team on offense is to score. In order to do that, the offensive unit must work well as a group. Players must successfully complete their assignments on each play. That is called execution.

When players do not complete their jobs, that is called a breakdown. If players forget what their jobs are, that is called a blown assignment. Breakdowns and blown assignments can result in the defense unexpectedly getting the football. That is called a turnover. An offensive team wants as few turnovers as possible.

OFFENSIVE FORMATION

There are strict rules governing how an offense lines up its players. The way an offense lines up is called a formation. Members of the offensive line almost always line up in the same way. The positioning of the backs and receivers can differ.

The center lines up over the ball on the line of scrimmage (see page 19). On both sides of the center are the guards. The two tackles line up next to the guards. Two more players, usually receivers, must also be positioned on the line of scrimmage. An offensive formation is legal when there are at least seven offensive players positioned at the line of scrimmage.

OFFENSIVE LINE

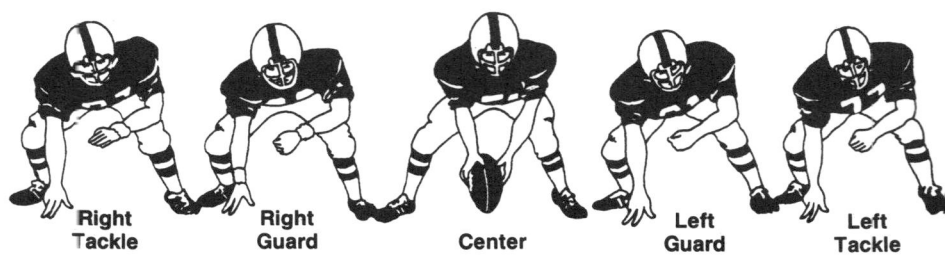

Right Tackle | Right Guard | Center | Left Guard | Left Tackle

Where those two additional players line up varies. Normally it is one player on each side of the tackles. A receiver positioned close to the tackle is a tight end. A receiver positioned far from the tackle is a split end.

The area on the field where the football lies is special. It is called the neutral zone. The neutral zone is from one tip of the football to the other.

Only the center is allowed to have any part of his body *in* the neutral zone. The other members of the offensive line must assume a stance behind the neutral zone. Otherwise, the offense will be penalized.

NUMBERING HOLES

The gaps between members of the offensive line are numbered. For example, the gap between the center and the right guard might be hole 1. That would make hole 3 the gap between the right guard and tackle. The gap between the right tackle and end would be hole 5. The area outside the end might be hole 7.

The gaps on the other side might be numbered 2,4,6, and 8, starting at the left of the center. One side of the offense is always odd numbers and the other is even numbers.

NUMBERING HOLES

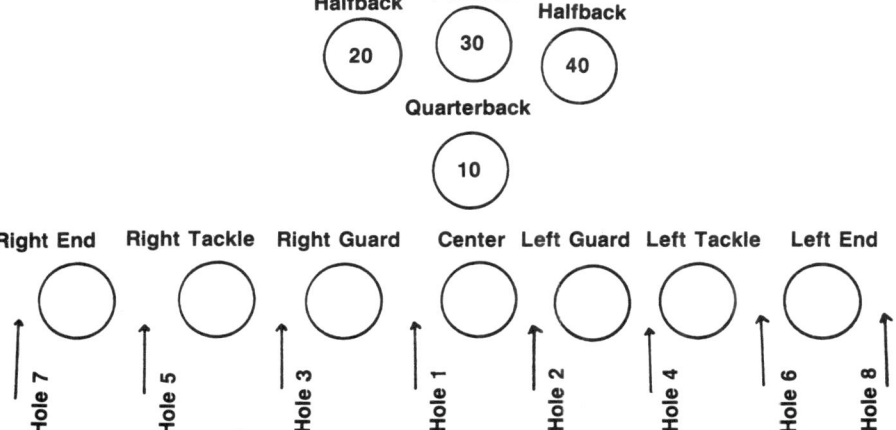

The backs are also assigned numbers. The fullback is usually 30. One halfback is 20 and the other is 40. The quarterback is 10, and so on. That is how plays are called.

A "43 Dive Play" is simple. The 40 halfback gets the ball and runs into hole 3. According to this number system, hole 3 is between the right guard and the tackle. The right guard and the tackle have preset blocking assignments for that play. The other players all have assignments too. That is how the offensive players know what to do on each play.

HUDDLE

After each down, the offensive players get into a small tight group to plan strategy. It is called a huddle. The quarterback is usually the only player allowed to speak in the offensive huddle. What play the quarterback calls depends on the down, the defense, and the ball's position on the field.

COUNT

In the huddle, the quarterback selects the play and the count on which the center will move the ball into the quarterback's hands. As the offense gets set on the line of scrimmage, the quarterback calls the play and follows with the count, which is the word "hut" repeated several times usually. If the count decided on in the huddle is "on two," then the ball will be moved on the second "hut." This way, the offense acts in unison and also gets a slight edge over the opposing team's defense.

CENTER-QUARTERBACK EXCHANGE

A snap is usually a short, quick, hand-to-hand exchange of the football between the center and the quarterback. Most centers use one hand to snap the ball. Your thumb should be near the laces and your fingers should point toward the ground near the ball's front tip. Turn the ball sideways as you snap it through your legs. This is so the laces will be against the quarterback's hands. The quarterback can then throw the ball without turning it.

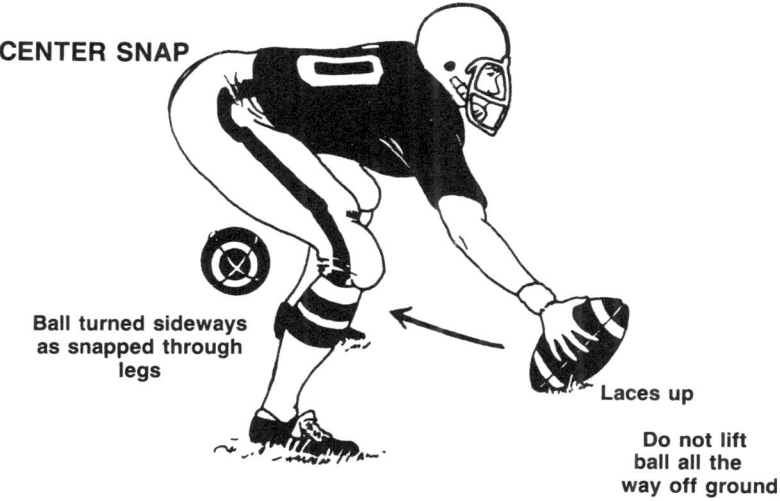

CENTER SNAP

Ball turned sideways as snapped through legs

Laces up

Do not lift ball all the way off ground

The quarterback takes the snap directly behind the center. Position your hands right under the seat of the center's pants. The heels of your hands should be touching, forming a sideways V, and your fingers should be spread apart. Right-handed quarterbacks should take the snap with their left hand palm up and their right hand palm down. The reverse is true for left-handed quarterbacks.

QUARTERBACK'S HAND POSITION FOR SNAP

QUARTERBACK CALLING COUNT

In either case, the ball should be snapped forcefully enough so that it hits against the top hand. The fingers of the quarterback's top hand can move easily into the passing grip on the laces of the ball, with the bottom hand providing support.

BLOCKING

When blocking, offensive players cannot use their hands to grab or hold opponents. They must block instead with their bodies, shoulders, and forearms. Knowing the count and firing out are especially important for the offensive center, guards, tackles, and even the tight end if they want to be effective blockers.

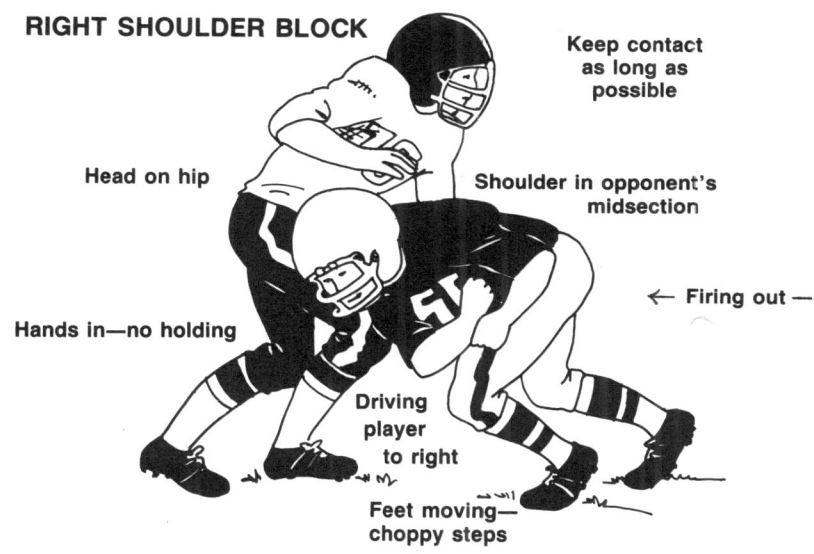

RIGHT SHOULDER BLOCK

- Keep contact as long as possible
- Head on hip
- Shoulder in opponent's midsection
- ← Firing out —
- Hands in—no holding
- Driving player to right
- Feet moving—choppy steps

Shoulder Block This is mostly used by players on the offensive line to clear a path for a running back who is carrying the ball. To shoulder block, drive right for your opponent's midsection. Take short, choppy steps and keep your feet wide apart and your head up. The crown, or top, of your helmet should not be used in blocking. To push the defensive player to the right, hit forward with your right shoulder, maintaining contact for as long as you can. The opposite is true for driving a defensive player to the left.

PASS BLOCKING POSITION

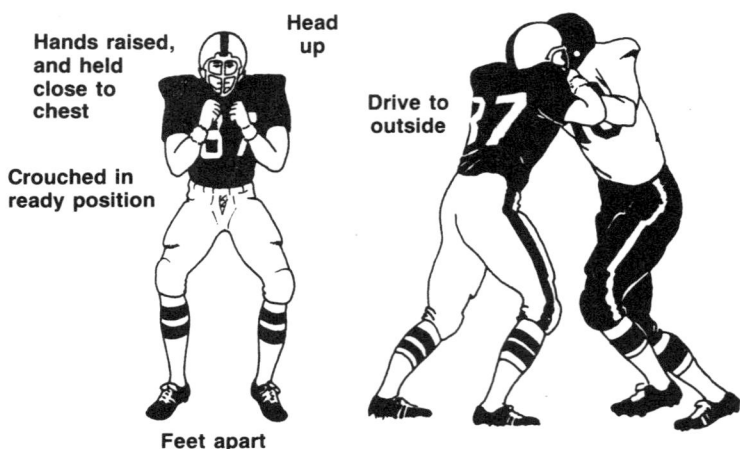

Pass Block This differs from run blocking in that you do not fire out or drive forward into the defensive player. Instead, you step back with your foot that's farther from the ball, set up, and allow your opponent to come to you.

Set up in a low, balanced position. Clench your fists and raise your forearms in front of your chest and away from your body. When your opponent comes into contact with you, maintain that contact. Keep your footing and always try to block a pass rusher to the outside—away from the quarterback.

HANDLING THE BALL

The first thing a back must learn is how to hold the football. Holding the ball improperly may result in a fumble (see page 17).

Bend your arm at the elbow until your arm forms a ninety-degree angle. Keep the elbow tucked against your side. That is where the football is carried. One point of the ball fits against the crook of your arm and is wedged against your hip. Your hand should curl around the other tip of the ball. The point should be cradled between your thumb and first finger. Carrying the ball with the back point away from your body can result in the ball popping loose if you're tackled.

HOLDING THE BALL

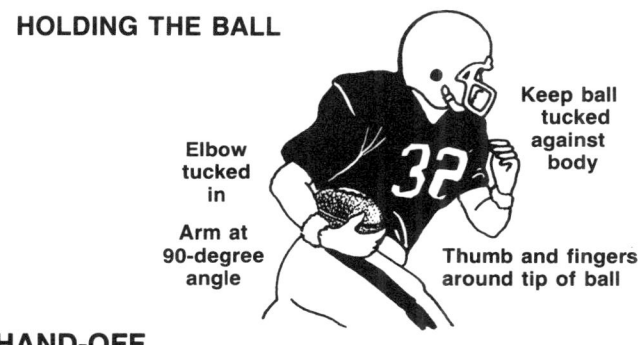

Elbow tucked in

Arm at 90-degree angle

Keep ball tucked against body

Thumb and fingers around tip of ball

HAND-OFF

A runner's hands and arms must be in a special position to receive a hand-off from the quarterback.

Suppose you're to be the ball carrier. You're going left and the hand-off will be to the left. Raise your right arm with the forearm across your chest. Keep the right arm chest high with the palm down. Your left arm should be across the abdomen about bellybutton high, with your palm up. Tuck your left elbow tightly near your body.

During the hand-off, the ball will be shoved into the pocket formed by your two arms. The tip of the ball should hit against your left elbow. That will keep the ball from sliding out. As soon as the ball is in the pocket, close both your arms over the ball to protect it. Your arms should stay over the ball until you're through the line of scrimmage.

To receive a hand-off on the other side, reverse the position of your hands. On a hand-off right, your right arm should be down across the stomach and your left arm up across the chest.

QUARTERBACK HANDING OFF TO RUNNING BACK

RUNNING WITH THE BALL

When running with the ball, try to run in a low, crouched position. Get your knees up high and keep your feet churning. Always move forward and try not to reverse your field once you start in a certain direction.

You can also use a "stiff arm" to ward off a tackle. But you must keep your arm locked at the elbow.

PASSING THE BALL

Hold the ball with your thumb and fingers curled around it near the back point. Spread your fingertips and rest them on the laces. Placing your fingertips on the laces will give the ball spin when it is released.

Passes should be thrown overhand, not sidearm or in a three-quarter motion. Step as you throw. Get your body into the throw and follow through by allowing your arm to continue forward after you release the ball.

On long passes, you should try to "lead" receivers so they can catch the ball without slowing up or stopping. "Leading" means throwing the ball slightly in front of the receiver. It takes practice to learn.

On short passes, especially over the middle of the field, throw the ball lower and harder. This allows receivers to use their bodies to catch the ball. It also makes the pass harder to intercept and keeps the defenders from the ball.

CATCHING THE BALL

To catch the football, pay attention only to the ball coming toward you and don't worry about what's happening around you. That is called "keeping your eye on the ball." Never take your eyes off the ball before it is in your hands. Receivers want to catch the ball so that the pass is complete. They should also try to come back toward a thrown ball to catch it.

Once the ball is in your hands, bring it close to your body to protect it. That way, it will not be jarred loose if you are immediately tackled. Never worry about being tackled until after you've caught the ball. After catching the ball, always turn up field.

PASS PATTERNS

Pass patterns are set routes a receiver is supposed to take. They often combine running straight and then breaking sharply to the inside or the outside of the field.

In a *square-in* pattern, for example, a receiver runs straight down the field, then cuts at a right angle toward the inside of the field. A receiver running a *post* pattern goes straight down the field, then cuts toward the center of the field as if heading toward a goal post. In a *flag* pattern, a receiver runs straight down the field, then veers off toward one of the end-zone flags on the nearer sideline.

A receiver running a *hook* pattern runs straight down the field at top speed to a certain spot, then "hooks" around suddenly to catch the ball from the passer. The ball should already be in the air by the time the receiver turns toward the passer. A *slant-in* pattern simply means the receiver "slants in" toward the center of the field.

To be effective in a game, pass patterns should be run over and over again in practice. It's really the only way a passer can get to know a receiver's moves and *time* the passes accurately.

PASS PATTERNS

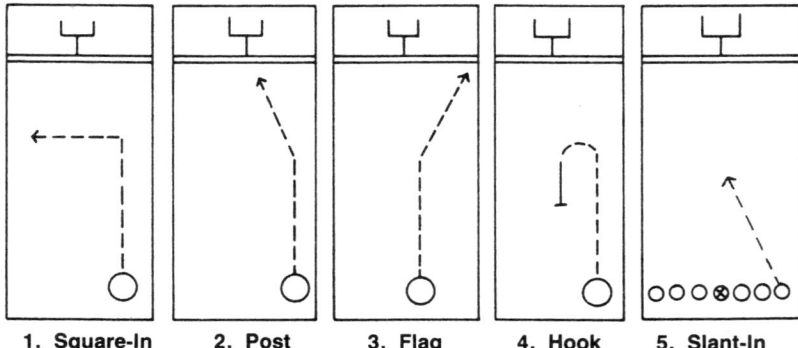

1. Square-In   2. Post   3. Flag   4. Hook   5. Slant-In

Defensive Play

While offensive play is very structured, defensive play relies more on reaction. The defense reacts to what the offense does. On each play, the offense knows who will carry the ball and to where it will be carried. The defense never knows in advance who will make the tackle.

Defensive players do have an advantage of their own. They can use their hands to ward off opponents.

TWO-POINT STANCE

Many defensive players, such as outside linebackers and defensive backs, use a special two-point stance as a ready position.

To assume a two-point stance, keep your feet spread about shoulder width. Bend at the knees into a crouched position. Your inside foot—the foot nearest the ball—should be slightly forward or up. The outside foot should be back, even with or behind the heel of the front foot. This makes if difficult for a blocker to knock you off your feet.

Your hands and arms should be out in front of your body and slightly extended. Your fingers can be open or clenched. Use your hands to ward off blockers.

TWO-POINT STANCE

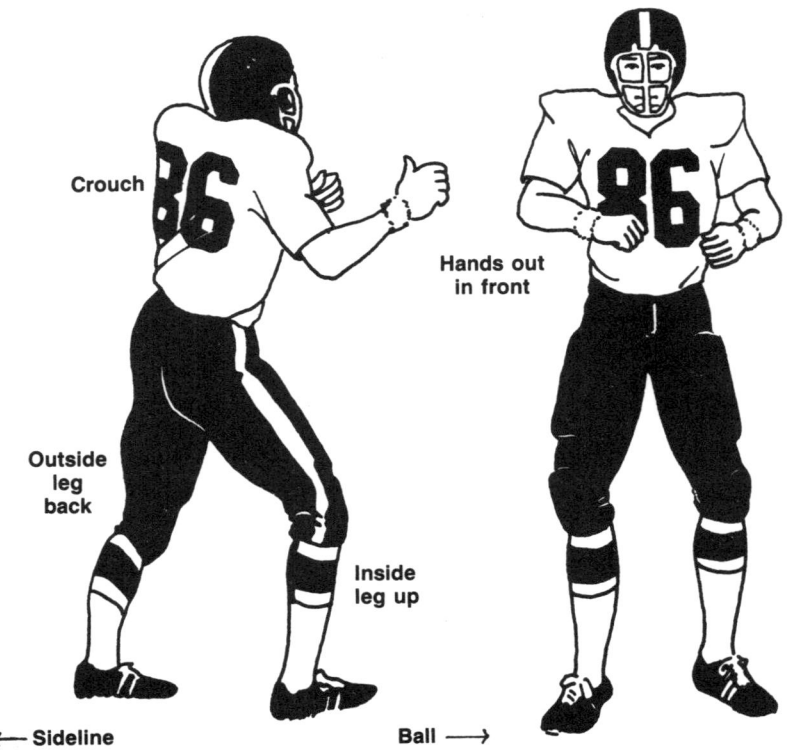

FOREARM SHIVER

Defensive line players use this tactic to ward off blockers and throw them off balance. To deliver a forearm shiver, swing your forearm upward from the hip, staying low as you step forward into a blocker. Keep your wrist locked and your fingers clenched. Your forearm should land against your opponent's chest or upper body. Use your free hand to push away or control the blocker.

However, do not hit an opposing player in the face or head with your forearm. That is illegal and will draw an automatic penalty.

CORNER PLAY

Defensive ends are normally responsible for corner play. They must not allow ball carriers to get around them to the outside. A defensive end has to "string out a play." This means forcing a back to run sideways as long as possible toward the sidelines. Stringing out a play allows pursuit, or would-be tacklers following the play, to catch up with the ball carrier.

TACKLING

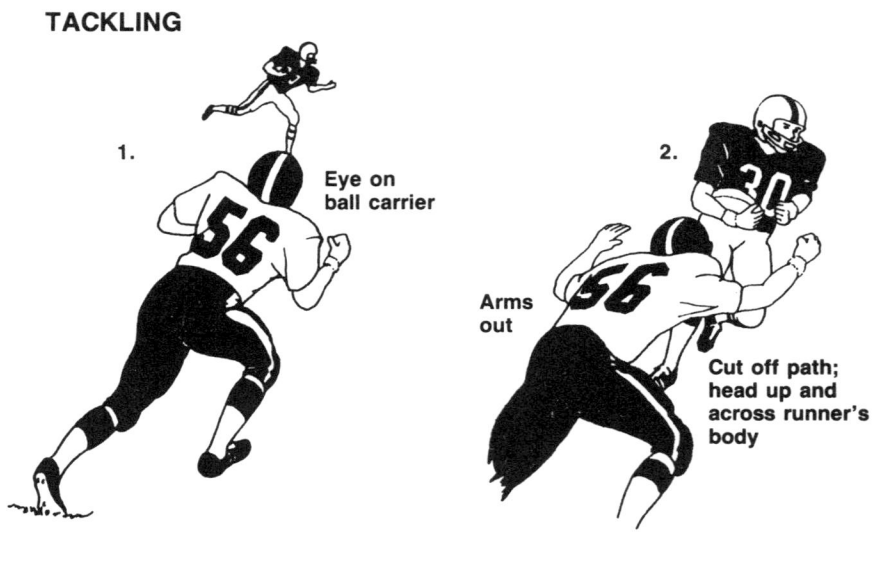

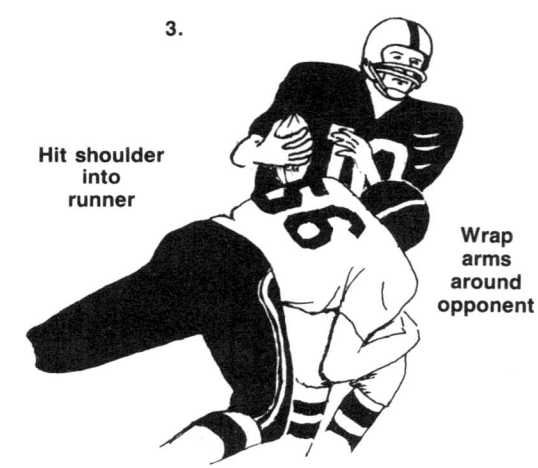

TACKLING

Tackling is probably the most dangerous part of football. Most football injuries result from incorrect tackling. Tackling should not be practiced or tried without the supervision of a qualified coach. *Only* a coach can teach you the right way to tackle.

SHOULDER TACKLING

The most common tackle is a shoulder tackle. It is like the shoulder block (see page 39). If the back is running right, tackle with your right shoulder (use your left shoulder if the back's running left). Drive into the ball carrier with your shoulder, putting your head across the runner's body. The idea is to cut off the advance of the ball carrier with your body as you make contact. Keep your arms out slightly extended to the sides.

As you make contact, wrap your arms around the ball carrier. Your arms should close around the legs, pinning them together. Keep your own legs driving.

Never hit into the ball carrier with your head. Do not close your eyes or put your head down. Always use your shoulder to make the tackle. And hit low, about hip high.

SHOULDER TACKLE

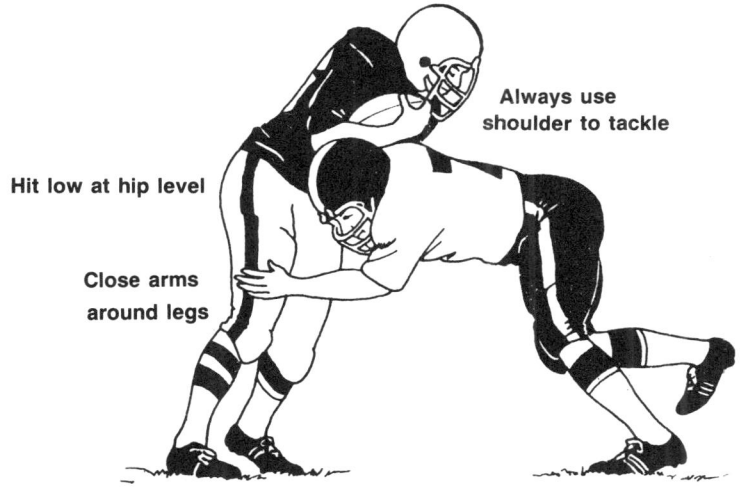

DEFENSIVE MAN SHEDDING BLOCKER TO GET TO BALL CARRIER

SHEDDING BLOCKERS

"Shedding blockers" means getting away from blockers as quickly as possible. A defensive player never wants to be tied up with a blocker too long. Get rid of a blocker quickly so you can then get to the ball carrier.

A forearm shiver is a good way to shed blockers. Using your hands to push or pull the opponent out of your path is another way.

PASS DEFENSE

There are strict rules for defending against pass receivers. A defensive back is only allowed to bump or hit a receiver once during a play. A defensive player cannot push, trip, or hold a receiver.

However, when the ball is thrown, it is a free ball. The defender has as much right to it as the receiver. If the defender can take away the ball fairly, it is an interception.

PASS DEFENSE

MAN-TO-MAN DEFENSE

Defensive backs in a man-to-man defense are expected to be almost like the shadows of the offensive receivers they're covering. The defenders go where the receivers go, and try to deny them easy opportunities for passes. To reduce the chance of a touchdown pass, a defensive back should stay between the receiver and the goal line.

ZONE DEFENSE

In a zone defense, each linebacker and defensive back has a certain area of the field to cover. When the play is a pass, go back into your area or zone. As you drop back, run backward or look back over your shoulder at the quarterback. When going back in coverage, you should never turn your back to the play.

Once you reach your zone, stay there. Do not follow a player leaving your zone.

PASS RUSH

On a pass play, it is the job of a player on the defensive line to pressure the quarterback. When you rush the passer, shedding the blocker as quickly as possible is a must. Moves such as a standing spin can also be used to get away from pass blockers. A standing spin is running into the blocker and then spinning off the blocker's body to one side or the other.

As you near the passer, get your arms and your hands up in the air. That forces the quarterback to throw over you. You may also be able to knock down the pass.

Defensive ends must remember not to let the quarterback sneak outside. They must rush from an outside-in angle.

PASS RUSH

Football Drills

TIRE PASSING

This is a drill for quarterbacks. It provides a target for passing practice. The target is an old tire. Tie a rope around an old car tire. Tie the other end of the rope around a tree limb so the tire hangs in the air.

Hold the football as if it were just snapped from the center. Then run backwards as if to pass. Your target is the hole in the tire. Try to throw the football through the hole. This drill can be repeated many times. It's a good way for a quarterback to become a more accurate passer.

TIRE PASSING DRILL

COUNT DRILL

A count drill is a firing-out drill for players on the offensive line. A coach tells the players a count—for example, "on two." The players get in their stance at a line of scrimmage. The count is called out. On the right count, the players fire out and sprint three to five yards. They stop and set down in stances again. A new count is called out and the drill is repeated. It continues down the field several times.

RUNNING TIRES

This drill is good for all players. Eight to ten old tires are laid flat on the ground. The tires are placed two by two (side by side) in two long rows. Players run down the two rows of tires, stepping in and out of the holes. One foot goes down one row of tires while the other foot goes down the other row.

This drill teaches football players to keep their feet spread and to get their knees high while running. It also improves agility.

RUNNING TIRES

GRASS DRILL OR UP-DOWNS

Up-downs are a conditioning and reaction drill. One player is a leader. The other players face the leader. On the leader's cue, all players start running in place, knees high. When the leader yells "hit it," all players drop to all fours (a pushup position). They then scramble back up to their feet as quickly as possible and resume running. The leader then repeats the call a number of times.

FUMBLE DRILL

This drill is a reaction drill for players on the defensive line. It should be coupled with up-downs. The fumble part is simply added.

FUMBLE DRILL

For example, a coach leads three players in up-downs. After several "hit it" calls, the coach tosses a ball on the ground while the players are on all fours. The coach yells "fumble." The players scramble forward, trying to gather in the loose football.

DUMMY SCRIMMAGE

Dummy scrimmage is an offensive team drill. Using padded bags (called dummies) or players standing in defensive alignments, the offense runs through its set plays at half speed and with no real contact. Dummy scrimmage is a drill used to help players memorize play assignments and to do those plays well.

TIP DRILL

The tip drill is for receivers, defensive backs, and linebackers. It takes three people to do. The three players line up in a straight line several yards apart. One end player (or coach) faces the other two and is the thrower or passer.

TIP DRILL

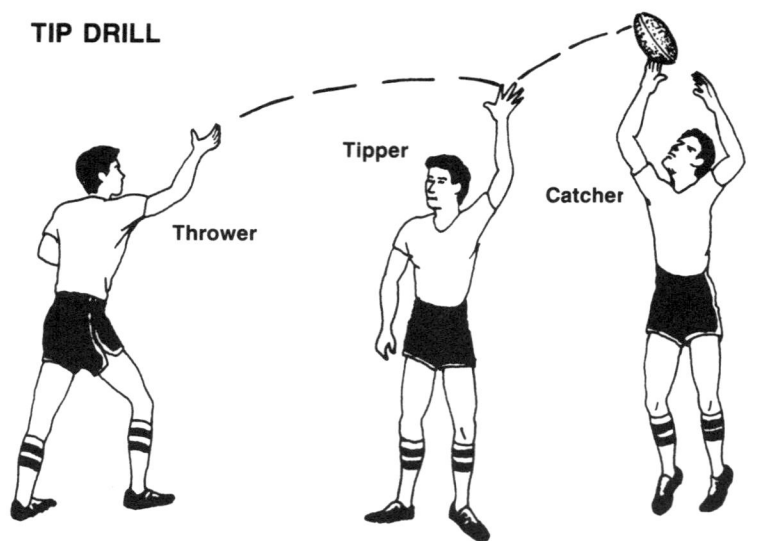

The passer throws the ball low enough so the player in the middle can slightly tip or deflect the pass. It is the job of the person behind the one in the middle to catch the tipped or deflected pass. This drill improves concentration and reaction to the ball. Players take turns catching the tipped passes.

TURNAROUND CATCH

This receiver/defensive back drill is done with two players. One is the thrower. The other is the catcher. The thrower has a football and faces the catcher. The catcher turns his back to the thrower.

With the receiver in this position, the thrower passes the ball to the receiver. As the ball is being passed, the thrower yells "ball." Hearing the word "ball," the receiver quickly turns around and tries to catch the pass. This is an excellent reaction drill that improves catching ability.

HIT AND SPIN

The hit-and-spin drill is a good pass-rush and reaction exercise for players on the defensive line. It requires the use of a heavy dummy and someone to hold it.

If you are the player to hit and spin, line up facing the dummy. On the call "hit," deliver a forearm shiver to the dummy. You can do this with your right or left arm.

After the hit, quickly spin out to one side on all fours. If you hit with your left arm, spin to the right. If you hit with your right arm, spin to the left. After you spin out, quickly get to your feet and sprint forward a few yards. Once you start sprinting, raise your arms in the air as if to block a pass.

HIT AND SPIN

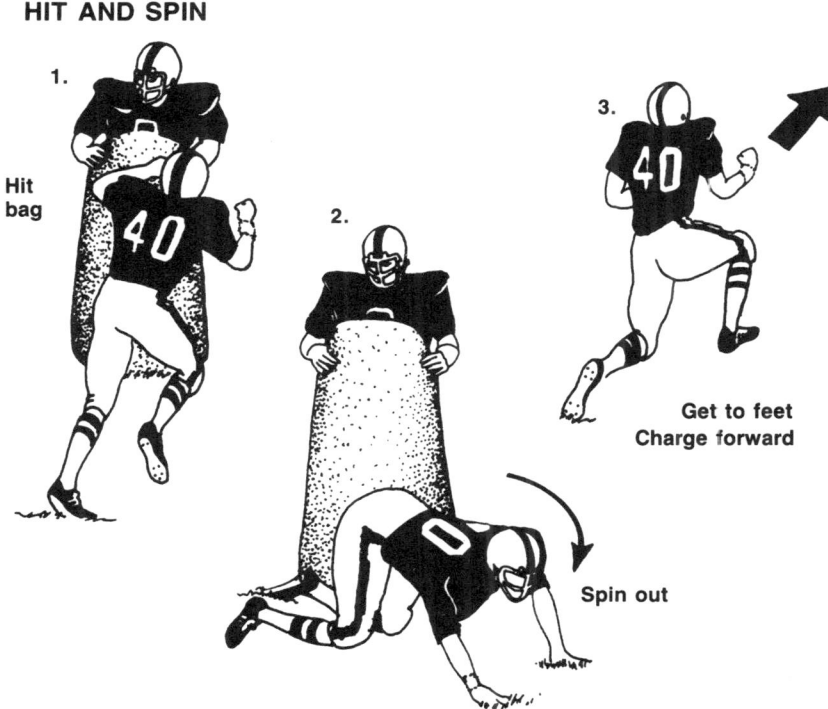

PASS-COVERAGE DRILL

The pass-coverage drill provides team passing practice for both the offense and the defense. Only line players are excluded from this drill. The offense calls a pass play in the huddle and then runs it against the defense.

The defensive linebackers and backs practice their various defenses, using zone and man-to-man coverage.

The offense has the advantage because there is no pressure on the quarterback to throw. However, this drill is usually run with a certain time limit for each passing play. The quarterback must throw within that time limit.

Touch Football

Touch football is a popular, light-contact form of American football that is played without special equipment. It can be played with any number of players where there is a fairly good-sized open space. In touch football, there is absolutely no tackling or rough blocking.

In one-hand touch football, a ball carrier is considered downed if a defensive player touches the runner with one hand. In two-hand touch football, a defensive player must tag the ball carrier with two hands at the same time to down the runner.

Most basic football rules apply to touch football with some exceptions. Usually anyone on the offense can be an eligible receiver. Players on the defensive line who are rushing must wait three to four seconds before charging in. They usually do that by counting "Mississippi's" out loud. A call of "One Mississippi" is about one second. Another exception is the way a team gets a first down. In touch football, the emphasis is on passing. Two or three complete passes in a series usually give a team a first down.

Sportsmanship

Despite its rough-and-tumble action, football is still a game. Always play within the rules. Tackle and block cleanly and legally. *Never* try to hurt or injure your opponent. Stay mentally tough, and your chances of winning will improve.

But no matter if you win or lose, no matter how rough any one game is, shake hands with your opponent afterward. Good sportsmanship is as much the sign of a "winner" as any victory on the field.

INDEX

Attitude / 23
Camp, Walter / 9
Conditioning
    calisthenics / 26
    distance running / 27
    sprints / 27, 28
Defensive Play
    corner play / 47
    forearm shiver / 47
    formation / 32
    man-to-man defense / 51
    pass defense / 50, 60
    pass rush / 52
    shedding blockers / 50
    tackling / 48, 49
    two-point stance / 45, 46
    zone defense / 51
Drills
    count drill / 54
    dummy scrimmage / 57
    fumble drill / 56, 57
    grass drill (up-downs) / 56
    hit and spin / 59
    pass coverage / 60
    tip drill / 57, 58
    tire passing / 53
    tire running / 55
    turnaround catch / 58
Equipment
    ball / 14
    helmet / 13
    hip pads / 14
    jerseys / 12
    mouthpiece / 13
    pants / 14
    shoes / 14
    shoulder pads / 13

Field (Dimensions) / 20, 21
Football
    history / 8, 9
    touch football / 61, 62
Goal Posts / 22
Kickoffs / 19
    scrimmage, line of / 19
Offensive Play
    ball handling / 40, 41
    blocking / 39
    catching / 43, 57, 58
    center-quarterback exchange / 37, 38
    count / 36
    formation / 31, 34
    hand off / 41, 42
    hole numbers / 35
    huddle / 36
    pass patterns / 44
    running (with the ball) / 42
    stiff arm / 42
Positions (Defense)
    backs / 32
    guards and tackles / 32
    linebackers / 32
Positions (Offense)
    center / 30
    guards and tackles / 32
    quarterback / 30
    receivers / 30
    running backs / 30
Rugby / 8, 9
Scoring / 15-19
Sportsmanship / 63
Stances / 24, 25
Time / 19